HALLSTATT, AUSTRIA
Adult Coloring Book

by Jordan R. Colton

The quaint and historic village of Hallstatt, Austria is one of the most beautiful and macabre places in the world. It is the home of the world's oldest salt mine, and was one of the reasons it was recognized as a World Heritage Site in 1997. Also hiddin within this old European town is also something that considered to some as horrific or disturbing.

Up on a hill overlooking Lake Hallstatt is the centuries old Catholic Chapel of St. Michael. With a cemetery known that is known throughout the world for a specific reason. This graveyard hosts a charnel house that holds over 1200 skulls of villagers on display for visitors to see. More than 600 of these skulls have been hand painted to display the name of the person, and their story.

I visited this village in 2016 with my girlfriend to see this house of skulls. We got into Hallstatt late in the day and the crypt was unfortunately already closed. We had no idea how beautiful the village was, so we decided to spend the night, and give it an entire day to explore along with visit the charnel house.

We loved it all, and consider Hallstatt one of the most special places we have ever visited. It's because of this that I chose to create a coloring book. I hope you will enjoy coloring this book and will have the opportunity to visit it or the exact replica of the village in Huizhou, China. (Google it!)

- Jordan Colton

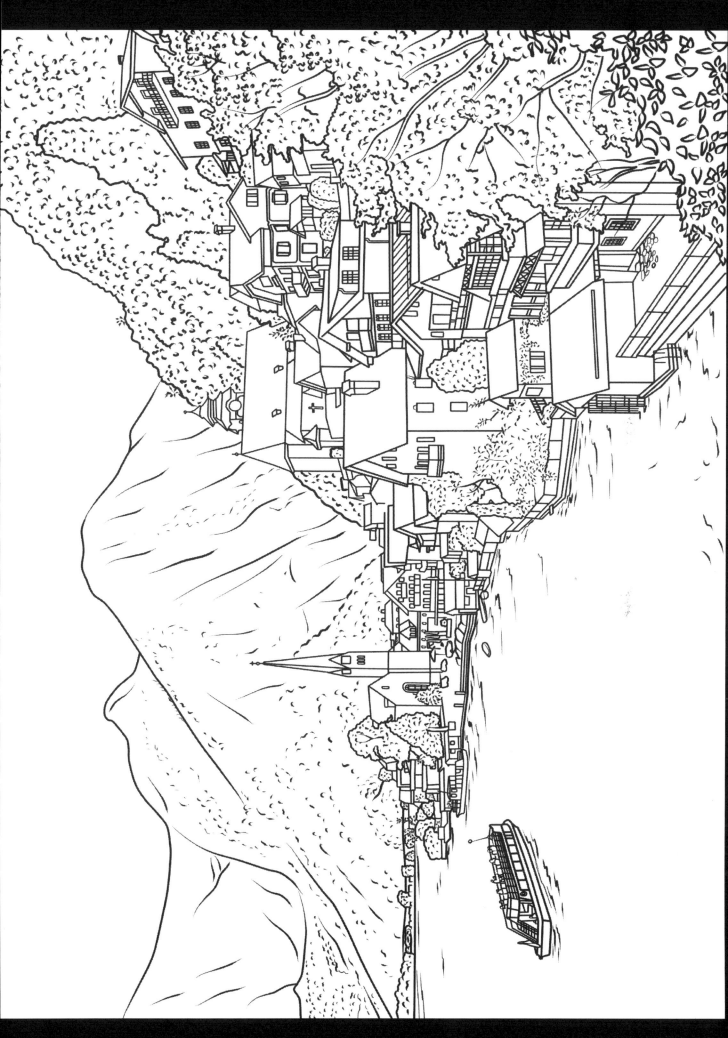

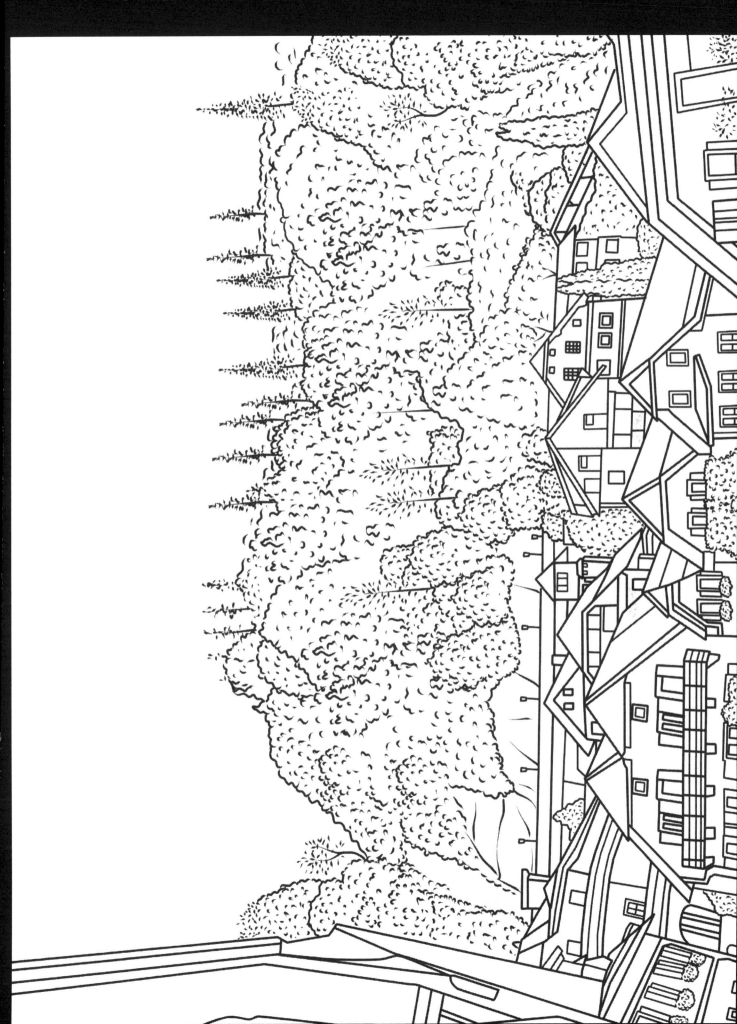

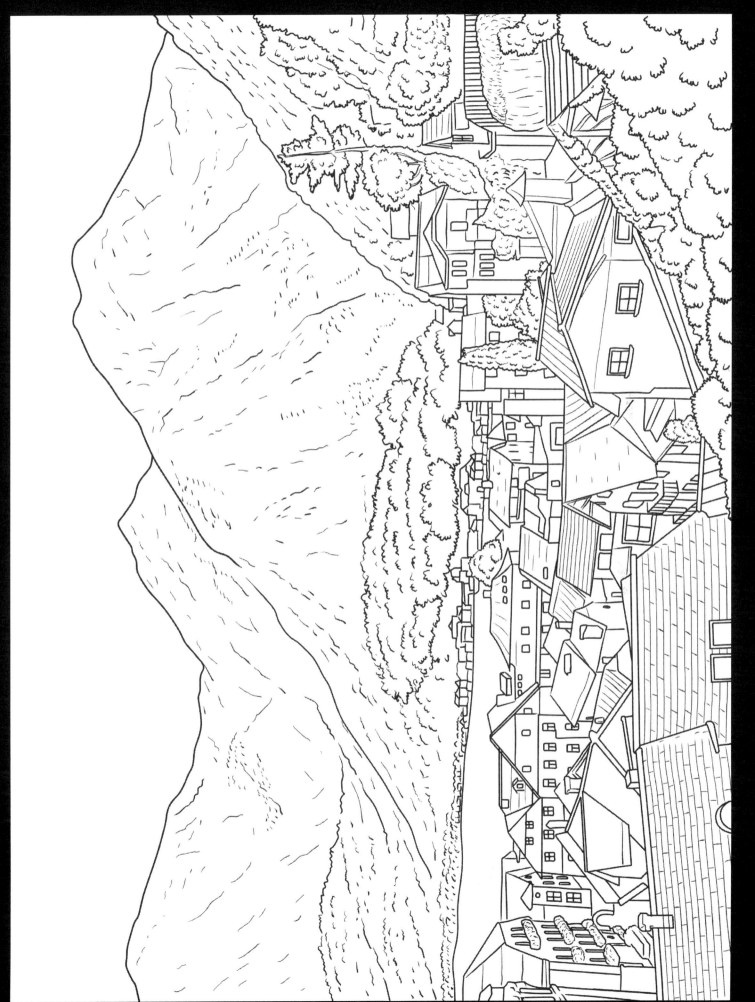

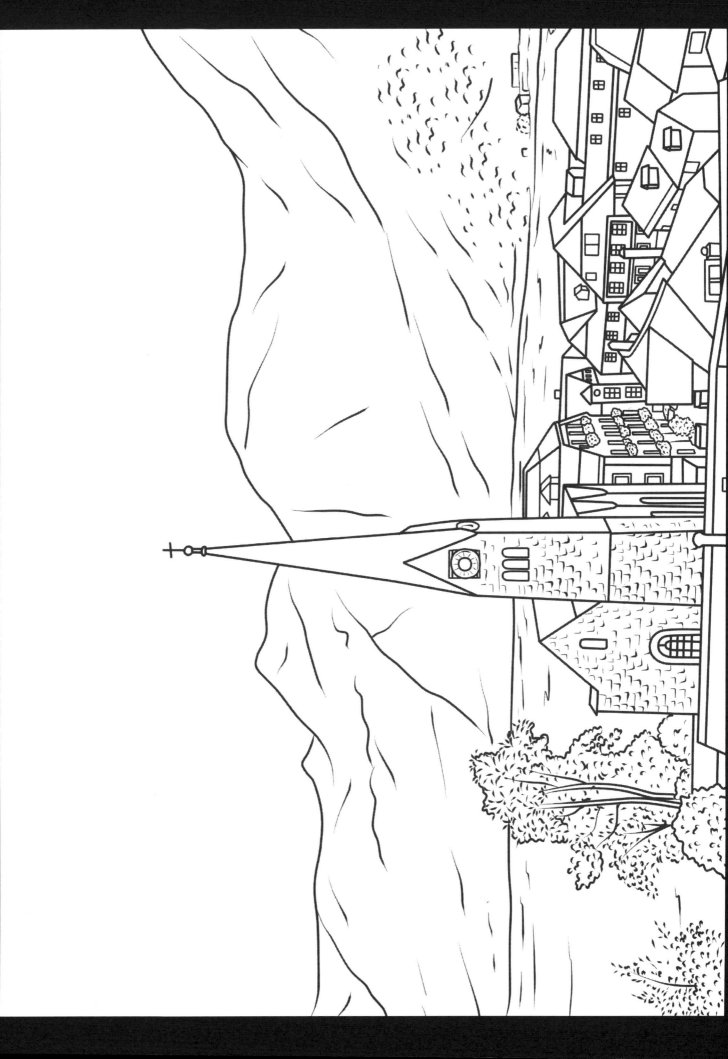

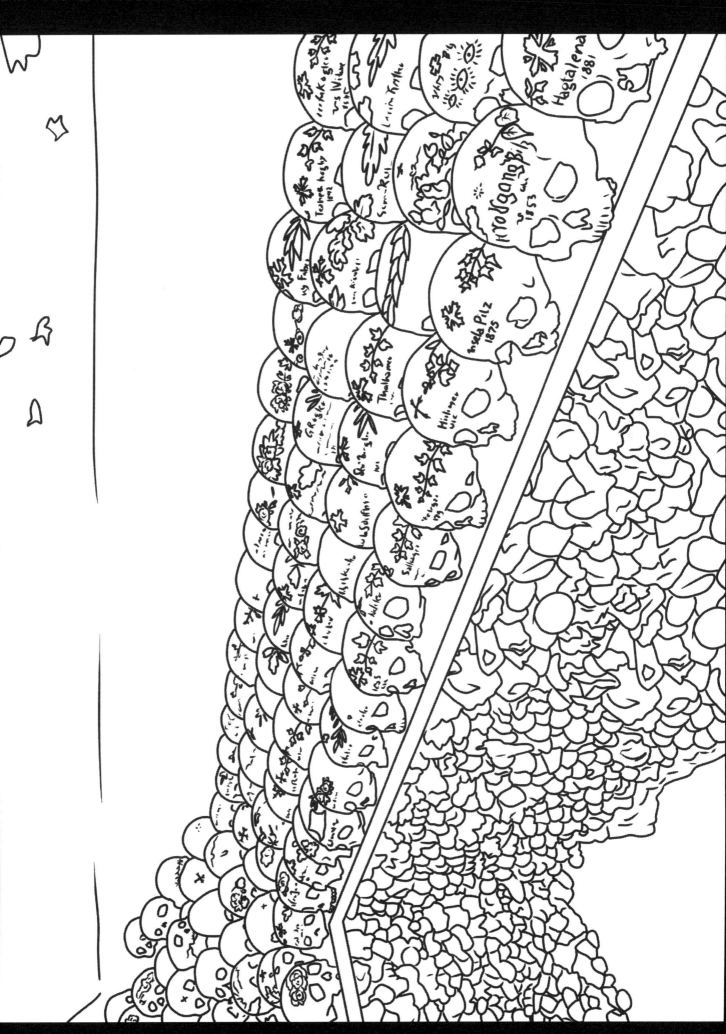

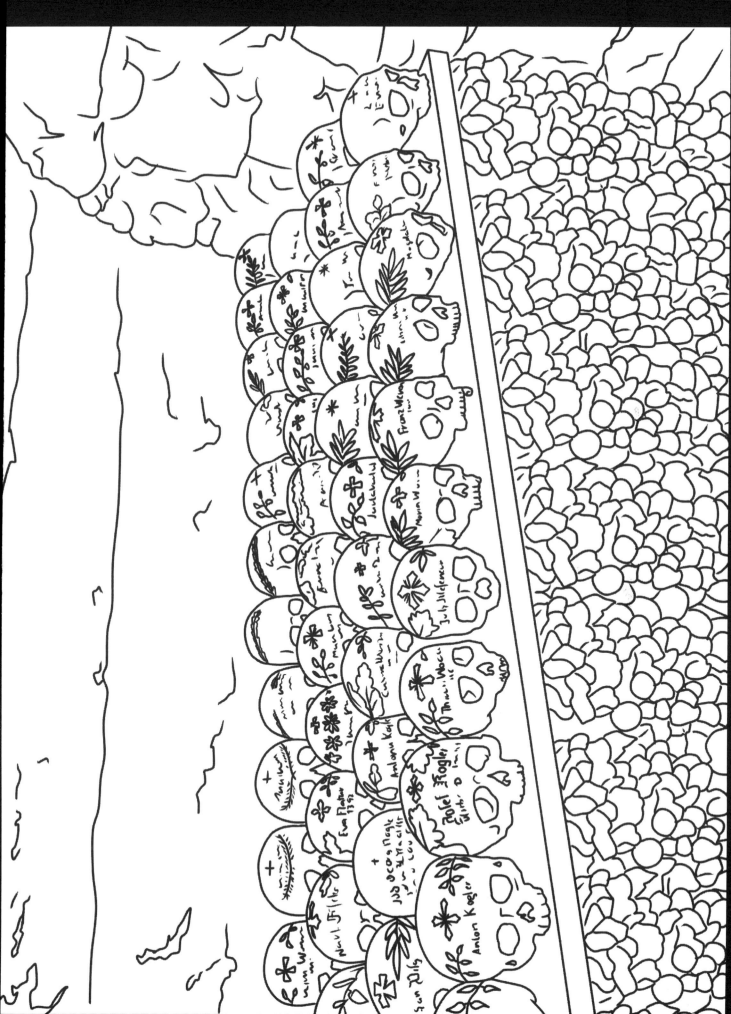

87058267R00043

Made in the USA
Columbia, SC
09 January 2018